WHAT'S YOUR STORY,

HARRIET TUBMAN?

Jen Barton
illustrations by Doug Jones

Lerner Publications ◆ Minneapolis

Note to readers, parents, and educators: This book includes an interview of a famous American. While the words this person speaks are not her actual words, all the information in the book is true and has been carefully researched.

Lerner Publications Company
A division of Lerner Publishing Group, Inc.
241 First Avenue North
Minneapolis, MN 55401 USA

For reading levels and more information, look up this title at www.lernerbooks.com.

Main body text set in Avenir LT Pro 45 Book 15/21. Typeface provided by Linotype AG.

Library of Congress Cataloging-in-Publication Data

Barton, Jen.
    What's your story, Harriet Tubman? / by Jen Barton.
        pages cm. — (Cub reporter meets famous Americans)
    ISBN 978-1-4677-7965-4 (lb : alk. paper) — ISBN 978-1-4677-8533-4 (pb : alk. paper) — ISBN 978-1-4677-8534-1 (eb pdf)
    1. Tubman, Harriet, 1820?–1913—Juvenile literature. 2. Slaves—United States—Biography—Juvenile literature. 3. African American women—Biography—Juvenile literature. 4. Underground Railroad—Juvenile literature. I. Title.
E444.T82B36 2016
306.3'62092—dc23 [B]   2015013891

Manufactured in the United States of America
1 – VP – 7/15/15

Table of Contents

Hi, friends! Today I'm talking to Harriet Tubman, one of the most courageous women in American history. I bet you're wondering why she's so important. Harriet, can you tell us a little about yourself?

Harriet says: I'm famous for helping slaves escape to freedom. In many parts of the United States, it was once **legal** for one person to own another. That's called **slavery**. Many black people were forced to be slaves. They had to work for white people without pay. Most slaves worked on farms in the South. In the North, slavery was not legal. Slaves who escaped to the North could be free. I led slaves north on a secret path to freedom. It was called the Underground Railroad.

Harriet Tubman spent many years helping people escape from slavery. By the time this photograph was taken around 1865, she had led hundreds of slaves to freedom.

Why did you work so hard to free slaves?

Harriet says: My parents and the rest of my family were slaves. When I was born in Maryland around 1820, I was a slave too. Most people who were born into slavery were slaves for their whole lives. I hated slavery. I wanted to be free, and I wanted to help others reach freedom.

When Harriet was growing up in Maryland, many white people in the state were farmers who owned slaves. These slaves worked on the land for no pay. They could not own any property or even choose where they lived.

What was it like to be a slave?

Harriet says: I lived with my family in a small cabin. It had a dirt floor. The cabin didn't have windows or furniture. It was too hot in the summer. It was too cold in the winter. I was always hungry. We had to work very hard all day—even the children. We weren't allowed to learn to read or write. I had to do whatever my master said. And he could sell any of us to someone else at any time. Two of my sisters were sold. I never saw them again.

Most slave families in the South lived in tiny cabins with dirt floors and almost no furniture.

Harriet says: I helped tend the crops in my master's fields. Sometimes my master sent us to work for other people. When I was seven, I worked for a nasty woman. I cared for her baby. If the baby cried, the woman would hit me with a **whip**. It was terribly painful. I got hurt in other ways too. When I was twelve, a white man threw a heavy iron weight at another slave. It hit me instead. After that, I had bad headaches and sometimes fell asleep in the middle of doing something. Things like this made me decide to run away on the Underground Railroad.

Many very young enslaved children took care of their owners' white children. This enslaved girl holds a white baby in 1855.

What was the Underground Railroad?

Harriet says: The Underground Railroad didn't use real trains or tracks. It wasn't even underground. But it was secret. It was made up of houses, or "stations." Those stations were safe places for runaway slaves to stop on their way north. Each station belonged to an **abolitionist**, a person who wanted to end slavery. Helping runaway slaves was against the law. But abolitionists gave food and shelter to runaway slaves anyway. They also helped the slaves find their way to the next safe place.

This painting from 1893 shows several white abolitionists leading a group of runaway slaves to freedom along the Underground Railroad.

When did you start working for the Underground Railroad?

Harriet says: In 1849, I escaped from my master's farm. I followed the Underground Railroad on my own, with help from abolitionists along the way. I reached Pennsylvania, the closest **free state**. But I knew I had to help others. So I became a **conductor** on the Underground Railroad. I made my first trip back to the South in 1850. Over the next ten years, I took nineteen trips.

Harriet helped take care of tired and injured runaway slaves on their way north. The journey was very long, and most escaping slaves traveled on foot.

What did you do as a conductor?

Harriet says: I helped runaway slaves find their way north. We didn't have maps, and most slaves had never been far from home. So it was easy to get lost. But I knew how to find my way by the stars. I knew which houses were Underground Railroad stations. I also knew how to fish and catch rabbits to eat. And my father had taught me which berries I could eat and which would make me sick. All those things helped on my trips.

Many safe houses on the Underground Railroad had hiding places for runaway slaves. Abolitionist Alexander Dobbin made this hiding place in his house in Pennsylvania. The sliding shelves *(left)* covered the entrance to a crawl space *(right)* where people could hide.

Where exactly did you go on your trips?

Harriet says: I always went back to Maryland. Usually I brought runaway slaves through Delaware. This tiny slave state had plenty of Underground Railroad stations. From there, we could get to Pennsylvania. But even in a free state, slave catchers could capture people and take them back south to slavery. So I led people farther north, to Canada. Canada did not let slave catchers capture people. The trip from Maryland to Canada took several days. We traveled through swamps, woods, and fields. Sometimes we walked the whole way. Other times, my abolitionist friends helped us get onto boats—or even real trains.

Harriet led runaway slaves from Maryland
into Delaware. Delaware was also a
slave state, but many abolitionists lived
there. Harriet kept going north through
the free states of New Jersey and New
York. Finally she reached Canada, where
runaway slaves could be safe.

CANADA

Miles
0 20 40 60

0   40   80
Kilometers

NEW YORK

ATLANTIC OCEAN

UNITED STATES

PENNSYLVANIA

NEW
JERSEY

MARYLAND

DELAWARE

Free states

Slave states

Canada

Harriet's route

How did the Underground Railroad stay secret?

Harriet says: We were smart. We only talked about the Underground Railroad in **code**, mostly in songs. We usually traveled at night and hid during the day. We hid under vegetables in carts and in old sheds. Or we hid in caves and hollow haystacks. Sometimes we hid in secret rooms in abolitionists' houses. If we had to travel during the day, we often used disguises.

Ellen Craft was an enslaved woman with very light skin. In 1848, she disguised herself as a white man so that she could escape from slavery.

Were you ever afraid?

Harriet says: Being a conductor on the Underground Railroad was dangerous business. Slave catchers were always on our trail. Slave owners were angry that I was helping their slaves escape. Some people even offered a $40,000 reward to anyone who could capture me. I knew if I got caught I'd probably be killed. But I never let that scare me.

$200 Reward.

RANAWAY from the subscriber, on the night of Thursday, the 30th of Sepember.

FIVE NEGRO SLAVES,

To-wit: one Negro man, his wife, and three children.

The man is a black negro, full height, very erect, his face a little thin. He is about forty years of age, and calls himself *Washington Reed*, and is known by the name of Washington. He is probably well dressed, possibly takes with him an ivory headed cane, and is of good address. Several of his teeth are gone.

Mary, his wife, is about thirty years of age, a bright mulatto woman, and quite stout and strong.

The oldest of the children is a boy, of the name of FIELDING, twelve years of age, a dark mulatto, with heavy eyelids. He probably wore a new cloth cap.

MATILDA, the second child, is a girl, six years of age, rather a dark mulatto, but a bright and smart looking child.

MALCOLM, the youngest, is a boy, four years old, a lighter mulatto than the last, and about equally as bright. He probably also wore a cloth cap. If examined, he will be found to have a swelling at the navel.

Washington and Mary have lived at or near St. Louis, with the subscriber, for about 15 years.

It is supposed that they are making their way to Chicago, and that a white man accompanies them, that they will travel chiefly at night, and most probably in a covered wagon.

A reward of $150 will be paid for their apprehension, so that I can get them, if taken within one hundred miles of St. Louis, and $200 if taken beyond that, and secured so that I can get them, and other reasonable additional charges, if delivered to the subscriber, or to THOMAS ALLEN, Esq., at St. Louis, Mo. The above negroes, for the last few years, have been in possession of Thomas Allen, Esq., of St. Louis.

WM. RUSSELL.

ST. LOUIS, Oct. 1, 1847.

This Missouri newspaper advertisement from 1847 offers a cash reward for the return of escaped slaves. Slave owners often hired slave catchers to capture and bring back runaway slaves.

Were you ever caught?

Harriet says: We had close calls, but we were never caught. We hid well and waded through cold swamps so the dogs would lose our scent. Sometimes, someone would get scared and want to turn back. But I never let anyone do that! I led more than three hundred slaves to freedom, including many of my family members.

Harriet helped many of her relatives escape from slavery. This photograph from 1900 shows Harriet *(far left)* as an old woman with some of her family members and friends.

What else did you do to fight slavery?

Harriet says: In 1861, the Northern states and the Southern states went to war with each other. This was called the **Civil War**. The war was partly about slavery. Many white people in the North wanted to end slavery. Many people in the South wanted to keep their slaves. At the beginning of the war, I was a nurse for the Northern army. Later, I worked as a spy for the North. I even helped plan **raids** against the Southern army. After the war, when I was older, I opened a home for people who couldn't take care of themselves. Many former slaves came to live there. I spent my life helping others.

As an older woman, Harriet stayed busy. She tried to improve the lives of other African American people.

How did your work make a difference?

Harriet says: When I guided people to freedom, I changed their lives forever. Those people could be paid for their work. They could have their own homes. They could learn to read and write. And when they had children, those children were free too. My work also helped convince many white people that slavery was wrong. After the Civil War, slavery was not legal in the United States anymore. I helped make that happen. I risked my life to fight for freedom.

Timeline

1820 Harriet is born in Maryland around this time. Because she was a slave, her exact birth date isn't recorded.

1849 Harriet escapes north on the Underground Railroad to Philadelphia, Pennsylvania.

1850 Harriet returns to Maryland for her first trip as a conductor on the Underground Railroad.

1857 Harriet helps her parents escape to freedom.

1861 The Civil War begins. Harriet works as a nurse and a spy for the Northern army.

1863 Harriet helps free almost eight hundred slaves from a Southern army camp in South Carolina.

1865 The Civil War ends. Slavery is no longer legal in the United States.

1913 Harriet dies of pneumonia, a lung disease, in Auburn, New York.

Glossary

abolitionist: a person who fought to abolish, or end, slavery

Civil War: the war between the Northern United States and the Southern United States, lasting from 1861 to 1865

code: letters, numbers, words, or symbols that stand for something else

conductor: a guide, usually a person in charge of a train or a streetcar. In the Underground Railroad, conductors guided people to freedom.

free state: a state where slavery was not legal

legal: allowed by law

raids: surprise attacks

slavery: the practice of one human being owning another

whip: a long, thin piece of leather with a handle that can be used to hit a person or an animal

Further Information

Books

Coleman, Wim, and Pat Perrin. *Follow the Drinking Gourd: Come along the Underground Railroad.* South Egremont, MA: Red Chair, 2015. Follow Old Ellie and Old Sam, two escaped slaves, on their path to freedom.

Evans, Shane W. *Underground: Finding the Light to Freedom.* New York: Roaring Brook, 2011. Travel with runaway slaves as they follow the Underground Railroad to freedom.

Moore, Cathy. *Ellen Craft's Escape from Slavery.* Minneapolis: Millbrook Press, 2011. Read about another brave woman who escaped to freedom with a clever disguise.

Websites

Discovering the Underground Railroad—Junior Ranger Activity Book
http://www.nps.gov/subjects/ugrr/education/upload/junior-ranger-activity-booklet.pdf
These activities let you imagine what it was like to be a slave and escape to freedom.

National Geographic Kids—Harriet Tubman
http://kids.nationalgeographic.com/explore/history/harriet-tubman
Learn about Harriet's exciting raid up the Combahee River and find out how one author walked in Harriet's footsteps.

Index

Photo Acknowledgments

The images in this book are used with the permission of:
© Pictorial Press Ltd/Alamy, p. 5; © Peter Newark American
Pictures/Bridgeman Images, p. 7; Library of Congress, pp.
9, 11, 23; © Cincinnati Art Museum/Bridgeman Images, p.
13; © Janice Huse, p. 15; © Louie Psihoyos/CORBIS, p.17;
© Laura Westlund/Independent Picture Service, p. 19;
© Mary Evans Picture Library/Alamy, p. 21; © MPI/Getty
Images, p. 25; © World History Archive/Alamy, p. 27.

Front cover: Library of Congress.